Bird Ringing
A Concise Guide

By Dawn Balmer, Liz Coiffait, Jacquie Clark and Rob Robinson

*This book is dedicated to the late Chris Mead who inspired
BTO birdwatchers and ringers for more than 40 years.*

Published by
the British Trust for Ornithology

British Trust for Ornithology
The Nunnery
Thetford
Norfolk
IP24 2PU

01842 750050
ringing@bto.org
www.bto.org
To report a ringed bird – www.ring.ac

First published in 2008
British Trust for Ornithology

ISBN 978-1-906204-45-7

Text: Dawn Balmer, Liz Coiffait, Jacquie Clark and Rob Robinson.
Design & Layout: O'Connor Design Consultants.
Printed by: Reflex Litho, St. Helen's Way, Thetford, Norfolk, IP24 1HG.

Front cover: Barn Owl by Richard Brooks (www.richard-brooks.co.uk).

Environment: This book, including its cover, is printed on Greencoat Plus Velvet - a paper which contains 80% recycled post-consumer fibre.

CHAPTER 01
Introduction 1

CHAPTER 02
Catching and Ringing Birds 9

CHAPTER 03
Understanding Movements and Migration 25

CHAPTER 04
Bird Ringing as a Tool for Monitoring and Conservation 39

CHAPTER 05
Getting Involved 57

CHAPTER 06
Frequently Asked Questions and Record Breakers 65

Acknowledgements 75

Introduction

WHY RING BIRDS?

For hundreds of years people have been fascinated by birds, with one of the greatest mysteries being their seasonal movements. In Europe people observed birds in particular seasons - Swallows and Swifts appeared in the summer months, wild swans and geese in the winter, but with the changes in seasons these birds disappeared again. Where did they go? Early theories suggested that Swallows hibernated at the bottom of ponds while Barnacle Geese, which spend their winter round the British and Irish coasts, developed from Barnacles. Thanks to ringing, we now know that birds migrate so that they can escape the harsh conditions of winter, or enjoy the longer daylight hours in summer, and find food all year round.

One of the best ways of understanding how and why birds migrate is to mark them individually so that we can track their movements. Our curiosity about bird migration led to the development of co-ordinated bird ringing. This involves fitting an individual bird with a uniquely numbered

metal ring so that the bird can be identified if found or recaught in the future. Although gaps still remain in our knowledge, thanks to bird ringing we now have a good understanding of the migration routes used by most species.

   As well as helping us understand bird movements, ringing has many other uses. For example, it can tell us how long birds live. We now know that some bird species (*eg* Manx Shearwater) can live for over fifty years. Through ringing we also know that most of the Blue Tits visiting your peanut feeder are unlikely to reach their third birthday, although occasionally they can live for ten years or more! When a bird is ringed we can look closely at its plumage, which often allows us to work out how old it is. We can also record measurements such as weight, which gives us information about a bird's condition. Ringing also allows us to monitor changes in bird populations from year to year and helps us to understand why some species are in decline and others are increasing.

   In this guide we explain how ringing has helped us to understand the complexities of bird movements, how birds survive life's hazards

Ringing has shown that British Swallows winter mostly in the Republic of South Africa where over 430 birds ringed in Britain & Ireland have been found.

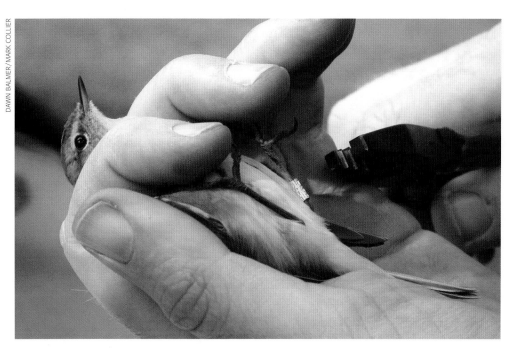

A metal ring being fitted to a Chiffchaff by a trained ringer, using special ringing pliers. Rings come in many different sizes to suit different sized birds. The photo on the left is a close-up of a larger ring that has been flattened out.

and how they may cope with the pressures of living in an ever-changing environment. Human impacts, such as changing land use, habitat destruction and climate change, are affecting birds to an increasing extent. As the following chapters show, ringing is a vital tool in monitoring the health of bird populations and in helping to plan effective conservation strategies.

HISTORY OF BIRD RINGING

The long history of marking birds to understand their movements begins as far back as 1219, when the Prior of a Cistercian monastery in Germany reported that a man took a Swallow from its nest and attached a small slip of parchment to its leg that read (in Latin), "Oh, Swallow, where do you live in winter?". According to this tale, the bird returned the next spring carrying an answering parchment reading "In Asia, in home of Petrus".

It was not until the 18th Century that the German ornithologist Johann Frisch disproved the theory that Swallows spent the winter hibernating in the bottom of ponds. To do this he had an ingenious plan: marking birds

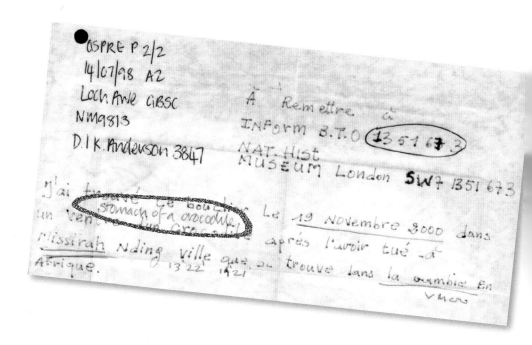

with threads dyed with watercolours. The birds returned the next year with the dyes still visible, proving that they had not hibernated under water.

Bird ringing for scientific purposes started in Denmark in 1899 when Hans Mortensen marked some breeding Starlings with metal rings engraved with individual numbers and a return address. Mortensen was trying to find out where the birds went; he made announcements in bird journals throughout Europe asking to be informed if any of the ringed Starlings were found. Mortensen's idea quickly caught on and led to the setting up of ringing schemes in many countries throughout the world.

Organised ringing started in Britain & Ireland in 1909 when two separate schemes were set up: one by Harry Witherby in connection with his magazine *British Birds* and the other by Sir Arthur Landsborough Thomson from Aberdeen University. The Aberdeen scheme came to an end during World War I, while Witherby's scheme was continued and was taken over in 1937 by the recently-formed British Trust for Ornithology (BTO).

RINGING TODAY
Britain & Ireland

The British & Irish Ringing Scheme is now one of the largest in the world, with over 2,300 trained ringers, and 2009 marks the centenary of the Scheme. Around 800,000 birds are ringed each year and by 2008 the total number of birds ringed in Britain & Ireland was over 35 million! Each year there are around

Each year the BTO receives details of around 6,500 dead birds. This recovery letter describes a ring from an Osprey that was ringed in Strathclyde, Scotland and found in the stomach of a crocodile in The Gambia!

Above: a ringed male
Pied Flycatcher with
food for his chicks,
right: a juvenile
Green Woodpecker.

14,000 reports of ringed birds – these reports are called recoveries. About 6,500 each year are of birds that have died, perhaps having been caught by the neighbour's cat, hit by a car, or shot by hunters. Some meet a stranger end, for example, a ring from an Osprey was found in The Gambia in the stomach of a crocodile and a surprising number of Black-headed Gulls have been killed by flying golf balls! These and other unusual recoveries are detailed in Chapter 6. Many more birds are retrapped alive and well at, or close to, the ringing site, often by the person who fitted the ring.

BTO ringers come from a wide variety of backgrounds and their ages range from 12 to 87. The majority of ringers are volunteers who fit their ringing in between families and/or day jobs, while a small number ring professionally as part of their academic studies. Most become involved in ringing because they have an interest in birds and their behaviour and want to learn more. Ringers feel a profound sense of privilege in being able to work so closely with wild creatures and contribute to our knowledge of them. Some spend only a few days ringing each year, others may be ringing most weekends; some ring on their own, but many are part of a local group – ringing can be quite a social activity. Many ringers focus on a particular project, ranging from studying the local Mute Swans or ringing owl chicks through to involvement with national projects such as Constant Effort ringing and Retrapping Adults for Survival (Chapter 4). Mist-netting for songbirds forms the 'bread and butter' ringing for most ringers, but others relish the challenge of studying species that are more difficult

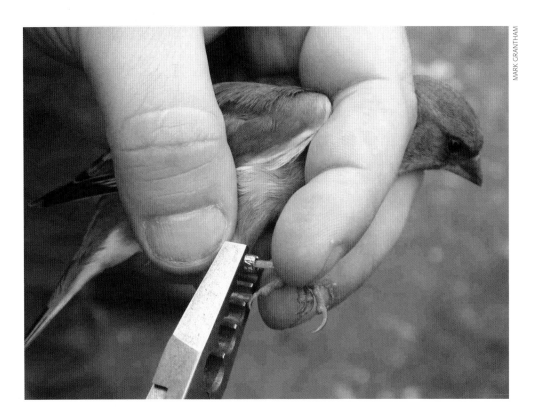

to catch, such as seabirds, waders or raptors (birds of prey). Ringers have a range of skills and talents that they bring to their hobby, and all make a valuable contribution whether by helping out carrying poles, keeping track of all the data collected, or in training the next generation of ringers.

All ringers are trained to very high standards; when ringing birds, the main priority is their welfare - great care is taken to ensure that the birds are not harmed in any way. For us to be able to draw valid conclusions about bird behaviour, inconvenience to the ringed bird must be, and always is, kept to a minimum.

When ringing birds, great care is taken to ensure that they are not harmed in any way. Ringing activities are regulated by law and all ringers undergo a rigorous training programme.

Throughout the world

Most countries in Europe, and many other countries around the world, have a ringing scheme. Within Europe, an umbrella organisation called the European Union for Bird Ringing (EURING) gives guidance and support to national ringing centres, and ensures data are recorded in the same way so that it is easy to exchange information, such as ringing details, between countries (www.euring.org). Increasingly, conservation and management issues need to be addressed at a continental scale and EURING co-ordinates international projects, for example, describing migration routes

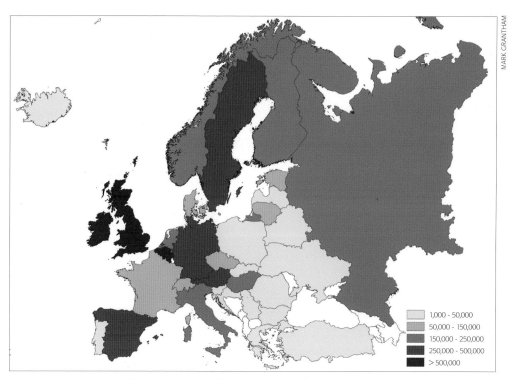

MARK GRANTHAM

	1,000 - 50,000
	50,000 - 150,000
	150,000 - 250,000
	250,000 - 500,000
	> 500,000

Map of European countries with Ringing Schemes. The different shades show the number of birds ringed annually in each country.

of waterbirds to help assess the possible spread of highly pathogenic strains of Avian Influenza.

In many countries BTO ringers have helped to develop a ringing scheme by organising special expeditions to look at particular species or conservation issues and by sharing the BTO's expertise in organisation and training. People from many other countries have also travelled to Britain & Ireland to receive training from BTO ringers.

RINGING IN THE FUTURE

Although we have been ringing birds for 100 years, there is still much we can learn from it. It is only by monitoring birds from year to year that we can record changes in numbers and try to understand why they happen – are they the result of natural events, such as a bad winter, or representative of longer-term problems (Chapter 4)? Ringing helps us to study what causes population change – the vital first step towards taking action to try to reverse declines. The simple placing of a small metal ring on a bird's leg helps us to collect this information as well as continuing to show us where, how and when birds migrate (Chapter 3) and to study changes in migration patterns (Box 6, page 29). But there is still more

to ringing than that – when we catch a bird we can also record its age, sex and measurements (Boxes 2 and 4, pages 16 and 23). We can then use this information to tell us about the health of populations and, for example, how males are doing compared to females and adults to juveniles. In addition to the ringing data, the measurements of birds are collected centrally so that analyses of data from all over Britain & Ireland can be carried out (Box 3, page 20).

A training workshop in the British Virgin Islands. BTO ringers have worked with many other ringers across the world.

As technology continues to develop we are finding new ways of collecting data to make the most of each capture. For example, adding a small radio transmitter tells us about the day-to-day movements of birds (Box 5, page 27), or clipping a small piece of feather can tell us where that feather was grown, helping us to establish where 'our' migrant birds go when they leave the country (Chapter 2). Even after 100 years of ringing there is still much to learn about bird behaviour, movements and population dynamics - areas where ringing continues to make a vital contribution. This book describes some of what we have learnt in the last 100 years, and looks forward to the future.

CHAPTER 02

Catching and Ringing Birds

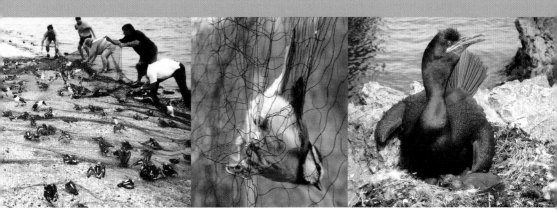

A great deal of important information can be gathered from ringed birds, but first, they must be caught! In some situations, such as chicks in a nest, it is relatively easy to catch birds, while others are more of a challenge. This can be because the birds are in inaccessible places (*eg* cliff-nesting seabirds), or it can be because they are good at avoiding nets or traps. Swifts, for example, are aerial acrobats, while crows are generally too wily to go near the traps in the first place.

This chapter covers some of the common methods used to trap birds, as well as the different ways that we mark birds and some of the information that we collect. The methods used to catch and mark birds cause them little more than a minor inconvenience. Marking can take the form of rings or tags attached to the bird, or they can be natural markers, such as DNA fingerprints, and ratios of the stable isotopes of elements such as Carbon.

CATCHING METHODS

During the early days of ringing, most birds were ringed as chicks in the nest or shortly after leaving the nest. The first report of a bird ringed in Britain & Ireland was of a Lapwing chick ringed in Aberdeenshire in 1909. Ringing chicks requires no specialist equipment but restricts the range of species that can be caught, and finding the nest in the first place requires considerable skill. However, ringing a bird in the nest is immensely valuable because we know exactly how old it is and where it hatched. Today chicks account for about 20% of all birds ringed. Many ringers also visit nests regularly to record how many eggs are laid and how many of the chicks survive to fledge from the nest. These details are submitted to the BTO's Nest Record Scheme (Box 1, page 14), thereby greatly increasing the value of the ringing record.

Bird Observatories and Helgoland traps

Bird movements are often most visible around our coasts, so to study them Ronald Lockley set up the first bird observatory on Skokholm in 1933. Others quickly followed and a network of observatories became established during the 1950s. Today there are 19 bird observatories, whose work is overseen by the Bird Observatories Council (www.birdobscouncil.org.uk).

As bird observatories spread around the coasts of Britain, people realised that if birds could be caught and ringed, rather than simply counted, much more could be learned. So there was a need to develop a method to catch the large numbers of birds migrating past. The answer came from ringers at the observatory in Helgoland, Germany, who developed a special trap to catch birds. A Helgoland trap is effectively a large funnel, built out of wire on a wooden frame, which directs birds into a catching box at the end. Helgoland traps are placed in valleys, along hedgerows or stone walls, or anywhere that migrants fly along a natural line and where vegetation camouflages the trap. These traps can be operated in a variety of weather conditions and are particularly useful at coastal sites where it may be too windy to use mist nets (see below). Helgoland traps are still used at most observatories today.

Mist nets

The greatest advance in catching birds came in 1956 when the first mist nets were imported into Britain from Japan. Mist nets are very fine, but strong, nets made from polyester or nylon that are stretched taut between

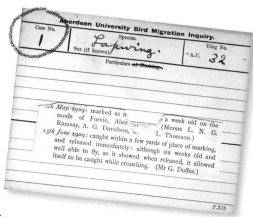

This Lapwing chick, ringed in Aberdeenshire in 1909, was the first report of a British-ringed bird. It was found at the same site five weeks after it was ringed.

HELGOLAND TRAPS
Birds enter the wire tunnel (left) and are directed into the catching box at the end (right).

MIST NETS
Above: mist nets, top right: a Blue Tit caught in a mist net, bottom right: a ringer extracting a Blackcap from a net.

two poles. They are designed to catch birds in flight and are usually dyed black, which makes them almost invisible, particularly in calm, dull weather conditions. Tight strings pass through the net horizontally to form 'pockets' in the netting into which birds fall when caught. The birds lie quietly in the net until an experienced ringer extracts them. Mist nets are very effective at catching a large range of passerine species. Mist-netting is usually done early in the morning when birds are most active; this can mean very early starts in the summer when dawn is at 4 am, or even earlier!

Catching flocks of birds

Specialist techniques have also been developed to catch flocking species, such as geese, waders and gulls. A 'whoosh' net (named after the noise it makes) is placed on the ground and released over a flock of birds using elastic cords. Cannon nets are a bigger version of a whoosh net, enabling larger numbers of birds, such as waders, to be caught safely. A net is placed on the ground and carefully disguised with natural materials such as seaweed or grass before being fired over a flock of birds. Ringers using these nets have extra training and work with an experienced team so that birds can be extracted quickly from the net.

Safety first

As with all ringing, the safety of the bird always comes first. The ringer ensures that nets or traps are checked regularly and that birds are ringed promptly and released in a safe place. If you find a net or trap with birds in please do not attempt to take them out as a ringer will be close by and checking the nets on a regular basis. It will take a ringer seconds to extract a bird, whereas unskilled hands may cause harm. If you are in any doubt about the legality of the ringing please ask to see a ringing permit and take the name of the ringer. You can contact BTO HQ (see back cover) to verify that they are ringing legally.

BIRD RINGS

Bird rings come in all shapes and sizes and are designed to fit comfortably on a bird's leg. The weight of the ring is tiny in relation to the daily fluctuations in body weight, which may vary by 10% or more. There are more than 20 different ring sizes and each species, from the tiny Goldcrest (weighing 5-6 g) to the Mute Swan (weighing up to12 kg), has a recommended ring size. Example weights of rings are given in Chapter 6. Specially engineered pliers are used to fit bird rings. They are designed so that the ring can be closed without putting any pressure on the bird's leg.

Most rings are made from a lightweight magnesium-aluminium alloy. Birds living in saltwater, particularly those using rocky shores or cliffs, have

NIGEL CLARK / SAM TALARICO

CANNON NET

Catching waders using a cannon net. Cannons fire the net over a flock of birds (1 & 2), the ringing team move to the net immediately after it has been fired to take the birds out (3-5), two Dunlin about to be ringed (6).

BOX 1 THE NEST RECORD SCHEME

Since 1939, volunteer nest recorders have been collecting data for the BTO's Nest Record Scheme (NRS), enabling us to monitor changes in breeding success.

Numbers of Linnets fell rapidly in the UK between the mid 1970s and mid 1980s. NRS data showed that the decline was due to an increasing proportion of nests failing at the egg stage.

Simply knowing that a species is declining is not enough to reverse the trend. Ringing and NRS data provide vital information about changes in survival rates and breeding success, giving conservationists a better understanding of the factors responsible for the decline.

Recording nests
Recording nests for the NRS is incredibly beneficial for conservation and it also gives you the chance to learn about your local bird populations in more detail. Contact the Nest Records Officer (nest.records@bto.org) or visit our website to learn more (www.bto.org/survey/nest_records).

Laying date trends
Trends in laying dates, clutch size, brood size and failure rates from the mid-1960s to the present day are updated every year for over 90 species and published on the BTO website as part of the Breeding Birds in the Wider Countryside report (www.bto.org/birdtrends).

For example, NRS data have shown that many bird species have started laying their eggs earlier, as a result of climate change. Nest records are also used to investigate how changes in land use affect breeding birds.

CHAFFINCH FIRST EGG LAYING DATES

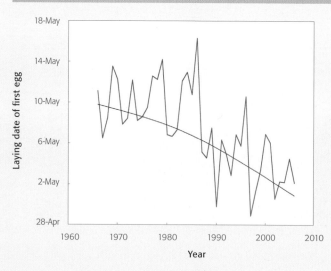

NRS records have have shown that Chaffinches are laying their eggs over a week earlier than they were thirty years ago. This is due to an increase in spring temperatures.

JEZ BLACKBURN

A selection of metal and colour rings. A variety of ring sizes are made by Porzana Ltd who supply bird rings and ringing tools to the BTO and many other ringing schemes worldwide.

rings made of a hard-wearing nickel-chromium alloy (incoloy) or stainless steel to reduce the effects of wear on the ring. The ring should last the lifetime of the bird, though one 35-year-old Oystercatcher is now on its third ring having already worn out two!

Each ring has a return address and a unique number that identifies the bird as an individual. Birds ringed abroad also carry this information, so if you find a dead bird with a ring, check the address carefully – it may have been ringed in another country. Birds from as far afield as Canada, Greenland, the Republic of South Africa and eastern Russia have turned up in Britain & Ireland. For information on how to report a ringed bird see Chapter 5.

OTHER MARKING METHODS

Using ordinary metal rings generally requires a bird to be recaught to check its identity, but if we add colour rings a bird can be identified without it being recaught as these rings can often be seen from a distance. One or more colour rings are fitted in a unique combination, or a colour ring with numbers or letters on it is used. This means that any birdwatcher with binoculars or a telescope can note the position and colours of the rings (or the inscription on the ring) and contribute to the study of colour-marked birds.

For some species the use of colour rings has dramatically increased our knowledge of their movements. For example, Icelandic Black-tailed Godwits spend the winter in the estuaries of Britain & Ireland, though some fly as far south as Portugal and even Morocco. By adding colour rings to their legs, researchers (with help from many birdwatchers) have been able to follow individuals from the breeding grounds to the wintering grounds and from one year to the next. This has shown that, amazingly,

BOX 2 A BIRD IN THE HAND

Ringing allows us to see birds close up, so we can record a range of useful information.

Species Identification: First the species must be identified. Some pairs of species, *eg* Marsh Tits (left) and Willow Tits (right), can be difficult to tell apart without close observation. Willow Tits have a pale-coloured panel on their wings, which Marsh Tits don't have. Marsh Tits have a white margin on their lower bill and tend to have slightly longer wings than Willow Tits.

Age: By looking at the shape of feathers, contrast in colours and how worn they are, it is possible to age birds as juveniles or adults. Juvenile feathers tend to be more pointed, looser and to wear more quickly than adult feathers. Growing a full set of feathers at once requires lots of energy, so juvenile feathers are not as strong as adult ones. In the Blackbird wing on the left, we can see both old brown juvenile feathers and newer, black adult feathers (circled). This tells us that this bird is a juvenile.

Sex: Some birds, *eg* Bullfinch and Blackbird, can easily be identified as males or females simply from plumage. The photo on the left is a female Bullfinch, the one on the right is a male. For other species, *eg* Goldfinches, there are subtle differences that can be seen by close obsevation, but in many others, males and females look the same and we cannot tell them apart.

Wing length: As well as providing information about the overall size of the bird, measuring the length of the wing can sometimes help identify the bird as a male or female, as in many species males tend to have longer wings than females. In some species, wing length can also indicate which population a bird comes from.

Weight: The weight of the bird can tell us how well it is doing, especially during periods of severe weather. Species that migrate a long way often build up reserves of fat before they depart from Britain & Ireland. Fat can be seen as a pale pink/orange colour under the skin. For more information, see Box 3, page 20.

Breeding Status: During the breeding season, birds that are incubating develop a brood patch. The presence of brood patches indicates that birds are nesting nearby and gives us information on the length of the breeding season. In most bird species only the females sit on the nest to incubate the eggs, so usually only the females develop a brood patch.

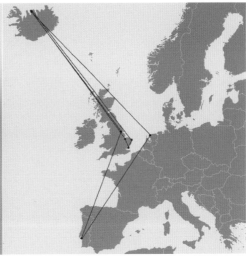

Colour-ringing Black-tailed Godwits has shown us that the male and female of a breeding pair tend to winter far apart – often in different countries. This map shows movements of a pair of Black-tailed Godwits in one year. The male (in blue) went to the Humber at the end of the breeding season, before moving to Portugal for the winter. He returned to Iceland via the Netherlands in the spring. The female (red) also moved sites in the non-breeding season, but remained in East Anglia for the winter. DATA SUPPLIED BY JENNIFER GILL.

despite often wintering in different countries, the male and female of a breeding pair arrive back in Iceland within a few days of one another.

Ringing birds with metal or colour rings gives us their location each time we see or catch them, but for some studies we need information more frequently, for example when working out how birds use different habitats in a reserve. Such information can be very valuable in determining how best to manage the habitats. One of the ways we can do this is by attaching a small radio transmitter to the bird when it is caught for ringing, and following its movements using a receiver. This technique is particularly useful for secretive species such as the Bittern, which are rarely seen. Bitterns live in reedbeds and marshes where they feed on fish, amphibians and insects. By following the daily movements of individual Bitterns, RSPB researchers have been able to work out their feeding requirements and how much reedbed is needed to support each pair. With this knowledge, habitats can be managed to ensure that the right mix of open water and reedbeds is provided for the birds.

For large birds we can use satellite transmitters to track their movements over the entire migratory journey. For species that migrate to Africa this has led to some exciting discoveries about the actual routes birds take, where they stop to feed during their journey and where they spend the winter. The transmitter is fixed to the bird (usually on the back) and can be

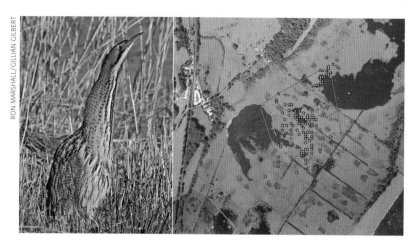

RON MARSHALL/GILLIAN GILBERT

Radio transmitters were used to track the movements of Bitterns. Each yellow star represents an individual fix or location. The red polygon shows the core home range where birds spend most of their time.

programmed to transmit a signal at regular intervals (*eg* every few hours). Currently, we can only use satellite transmitters on larger birds such as Osprey, Marsh Harrier and Honey Buzzard (Box 5, page 27). However, it is likely that we will be able to follow more species in this way in the future as smaller and lighter transmitters are developed.

Many other new technologies are being used by ringers to help improve our understanding of the movements and lifestyles of birds. For example, data loggers (small, computerised tags that record position, temperature, *etc*) have been used to work out how far seabirds travel from their breeding colonies to find food and how deep they dive. By attaching data loggers to Shags, ringers have learned that older, more experienced birds are better at finding food for their chicks, particularly when food is scarce.

PIT (Passive Integrated Transponder) tags, similar to the microchips used to identify pet dogs and cats, can be used to record how often birds return to a particular spot, such as their nest. In addition to the normal metal ring, a second ring, with a unique chip, is fitted to the bird. A scanner fixed near the nest records each visit by the chipped parent bird. This allows us to build up a picture of the number of visits and time spent on the nest.

As in humans, birds have a unique DNA 'finger-print', which can be used to tell us who is related to whom, as well as how closely different populations are related to each other. For a long time individuals of most bird species were assumed to have only one partner. However, DNA studies have shown that many young are not in fact fathered by the male that helped raise them, but instead result from the female mating with other males (males may also mate with more than one female). For example, a study of a Reed Bunting population found that 55% of chicks were not fathered by the pair male. Genetic analysis can also give some insights into migratory movements of different populations. For example, differences in DNA enabled researchers

Newer technologies complement ringing and help us learn even more about birds. For example, fitting data loggers to seabirds such as this Shag (right) can tell us about their feeding habits.

BOX 3 WEIGHT CHANGES IN BLACKBIRDS

Analysis of the national ringing dataset for Blackbirds has shown that they change their weight both throughout the year and during the day depending on whether they are more at risk from starvation, or from predators such as Sparrowhawks.

If a bird stores very little fat it will risk starvation, but if it stores too much, the extra weight may make it slower and more vulnerable to predators. Birds also risk encountering predators while they are feeding (when they are less vigilant) so spending more time feeding also increases the risk of being caught by a predator.

Seasonal changes: Overall, adult Blackbirds are heavier than juveniles and males are heavier than females. However, all Blackbirds increase their fat stores in winter when they need more energy to cope with the cold weather and long nights when they are unable to feed.

Daily changes: A bird's body weight also varies through the day, or with changing conditions. Birds generally lose weight overnight when they are unable to feed.

AVERAGE MONTHLY BODY WEIGHT

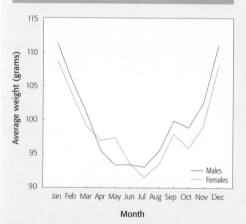

Females increase in weight in the breeding season when they are laying eggs. The apparent increase in September is the result of larger, Scandinavian birds passing through.

DAILY BODY WEIGHT CHANGES

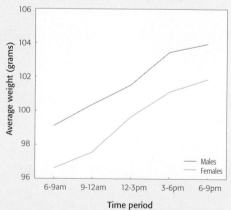

Birds caught early in the day tend to be light because they have lost weight overnight when they were unable to feed. Their weight increases during the day as they are able to feed and build up their fat reserves to last them through the following night.

STEVE ROUND

MIKE MCGRADY

PIT (Passive Integrated Transponder) tags, similar to the microchips used to identify pet dogs and cats, have been used to learn about the movements of Peregrines. In addition to the normal metal ring, a second small ring, with a unique chip (inset), is fitted to the bird.

in Sweden to distinguish between two races of Willow Warblers with different migratory behaviour.

The origins of birds can also be studied by looking at stable isotopes, which are naturally-occurring varieties of elements, such as Hydrogen or Carbon, whose relative proportions vary in different places. When animals (including humans) eat or drink they incorporate these isotopes into their growing body tissues, such as hair, feathers and claws. When birds move between different areas they carry with them information about the places they have visited (*ie* the stable isotope ratios in their body tissues). By taking a small sample of a bird's feather or claw tip after it has moved to a new area it is possible to analyse the ratio of stable isotopes in it, which allows us to work out where the bird grew those body tissues. See Box 6, page 29 for an example of how stable isotope ratios can be used to understand patterns of migration.

COLLECTION AND SUBMISSION OF RINGING DATA

We can learn much more from a bird in the hand than from simply looking at it in the field (Box 2, page 16). For example, we can use measurements to investigate differences between sexes and age groups. In some species ageing and sexing individual birds is relatively easy. For example, birdwatchers know that juvenile Starlings have a pale brown

No. of Ring.	Date.	Name of Bird.	Place where Ringed.	Remark.	Name of Ringer.	No. of Schedule.
Extra Large 12	28.5.10	Heron	near Cheadle Staffs 152·59N 1 59W	nestling ad 10.11.	Masefield	380

DETAILS OF RECOVERY.

Book of Recoveries.	Date of Recovery.	Name of Finder.	Place where Recovered.	Remarks.	Published in B.B.
111.	.10.15.	a. g. bowne her the field"	Church Stretton. 5232N 2 49W	Shot by a local keeper.	IX, 269

In the early days of the Ringing Scheme details of each bird were recorded on an individual 'Schedule'. The one above shows a Heron, ringed in the nest in May 1910, and later shot by a gamekeeper in October 1915.

Ringers now use a specially designed computer package to enter all their records, and email the information directly to BTO HQ. Each row shows a different record of a bird. The package was written by volunteer ringer Mark Cubitt.

plumage that is very different from the glossy, dark feathers of the adults. Similarly, many people know that female Blackbirds are brown, while the males are black. For other species determining the age and sex is much more difficult and can only be done with a bird in the hand. Ringers need to learn different characteristics for different species. Ageing a bird often involves looking at plumage differences, such as the contrast in colour between juvenile feathers and newly-grown adult ones (Box 4, page 23), or the amount of wear on the feathers. In some species subtle plumage differences, or the length of the wing, can help to sex a bird. Certain pairs of species, such as Willow Warbler and Chiffchaff, or Willow Tit and Marsh Tit, can be difficult to tell apart without looking at them closely when they have been caught. For some rarer species, such as many warblers, species identification can also be difficult, but can be worked out by taking measurements of the bird.

Ringers carefully record details of each bird and enter the records into a specially designed computer package. The ringing data are sent to BTO HQ and incorporated into the main database to become available for analysis. An example of how useful this information can be is shown in Box 3, page 20.

BOX 4 PLUMAGE AND MOULT

Looking at plumage and understanding patterns of moult allows ringers to age birds.

MOULT IN THE ROBIN
(1) a bird that has just left the nest, (2) a bird in post-juvenile moult, (3) after completing its post-juvenile moult the bird will look like this adult Robin.

First feathers

After birds hatch they grow their feathers as quickly as possible so that they are able to fly and thereby have more chance of avoiding predation. The first feathers are generally weak and of poor quality. Over the first few months of a bird's life some or all of these feathers are gradually replaced with stronger, better-quality ones. This is most obvious in species such as the Robin, which changes from a mottled brown colour to the red breast we are familiar with. This process is known as 'post-juvenile moult'.

Ageing birds using plumage

In many juveniles only some of the feathers are moulted. The remaining juvenile feathers may differ from the newer adult feathers in colour, texture, the amount of wear or shape. This allows us to distinguish first-year birds from adults. Some birds (eg gulls) have distinctive immature plumage for two or more years.

Annual Moult

Adult birds renew their feathers on a regular basis. For most species this happens after the breeding season because their feathers have become very worn as they flew in and out of the nest to feed their young.

■ Most birds will replace just a few feathers at a time and remain able to fly.
■ Some species, particularly waterbirds, lose most of their main flight feathers at the same time

and become flightless for a period, during which they are vulnerable to predators. Some species, particularly waterfowl, migrate to an area where there are few predators so that they can moult safely (Chapter 3).

■ Large birds, such as seabirds and raptors, may replace just a few flight feathers each year and it can take up to nine years before they have completely renewed their feathers.

■ Many birds also moult some body feathers before breeding; their breeding plumage may make them more attractive to the opposite sex, or help to camouflage them on the nest.

The Great Tit on the left is a first-year, and the one on the right is an adult. We can tell by looking at the circled feathers, which are duller and more pointed on the left. The younger bird still has some juvenile feathers, whereas the adult bird (right) has moulted them all and grown new adult feathers.

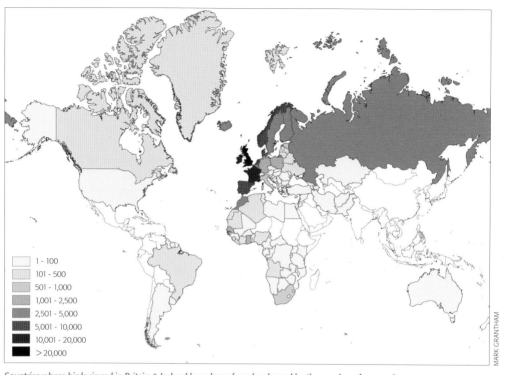

Countries where birds ringed in Britain & Ireland have been found, coloured by the number of recoveries.

MARK GRANTHAM

Legend:
- 1 - 100
- 101 - 500
- 501 - 1,000
- 1,001 - 2,500
- 2,501 - 5,000
- 5,001 - 10,000
- 10,001 - 20,000
- > 20,000

Ring recoveries

Recoveries are reports of ringed birds that are either found dead, or recaught away from where they were ringed. For the first 50 years of ringing in Britain & Ireland virtually all recoveries were dead birds found by members of the public. But as the Ringing Scheme has grown, many more birds are being recaught by ringers. The recovery rate (number of recoveries reported per 100 birds ringed) varies greatly from species to species. Large, conspicuous birds such as geese and swans have the highest recovery rates (up to 56%), whereas small, secretive birds that avoid human habitation (such as warblers) have the lowest recovery rates (as low as 0.2%). Rates are also high for birds such as ducks and geese that are shot by humans for sport/food and for many garden birds that are killed by cats and brought into the house. Birds killed by collision with cars or windows are also more conspicuous than those dying in woods or fields. Chapter 6 lists species with the highest recovery rates as well as common causes of mortality. However, the number of ringed birds being found has declined in recent years, so each bird found is more important than ever. If you do find a bird with a ring on it, see Chapter 5 for how to report it.

CHAPTER 03

Understanding Movements and Migration

Our reasons for ringing birds have changed over time. When scientific ringing began at the turn of the 20th Century the main interest was to find out where birds went. We have now answered many of these questions. For example, we now know that our wintering Starlings come from the Baltic States, and rather than hibernating in ponds (as was once thought) our Swallows winter in southern Africa. Today the focus of bird ringing is to monitor bird populations and understand reasons for population changes (Chapter 4). However, many questions about migration remain unanswered and even now we still lack basic information on both the routes and destinations of some of our migrants that go to Africa for the winter.

Many birds move to different areas to increase their chances of survival. Some migrate south each year for the winter, while others may only move when the weather becomes particularly cold, or in search of food.

JILL PAKENHAM

Many of the Whooper Swans that breed in Iceland migrate to Britain & Ireland for the winter.

One of the consequences of global climate change is that birds' breeding and wintering ranges may change, as may their patterns of migratory movements. Understanding migratory movements is crucial in predicting how migratory species are able to respond to climate change. This chapter discusses the different types of bird movement and how ringing can help us to understand them. As described in Chapter 2, newer technologies can be used to complement ringing and help us learn even more about bird movements. An example is shown in Box 5, opposite. The use of such technologies is already expanding and is likely to play a larger part in our studies of bird movement in the future, supplementing the information we continue to gain from metal ringing.

SEASONAL MIGRATION

For many bird species food resources vary seasonally. Young, growing birds require relatively high amounts of protein from insects and other animal prey. Many of the migrants that visit Britain & Ireland during the summer are insectivorous. During the spring and summer birds breeding here can take advantage of the abundant insects and long daylight hours for feeding. However, as autumn approaches and the supply of insects decreases they must fly south to find new sources of food. Similarly, many birds that spend the summer in more northerly regions feeding on plants, seeds and invertebrates fly south in the autumn to Britain & Ireland and other parts of Europe, before their feeding sites become frozen or covered in snow. As our climate changes, migration patterns may also change (Box 6, page 29).

BOX 5 SATELLITE TRACKING OF RAPTOR MIGRATION

Large birds can be fitted with satellite tags, helping us learn more about their movements.

By 1916 persecution had driven the British Osprey population to extinction. In 1954 a single pair (thought to be of Scandinavian origin) returned to Scotland and began breeding in the RSPB reserve at Loch Garten. Since then the species has gradually recolonized Scotland. 2001 saw the first successful nesting attempts in England, by naturally recolonizing birds in the Lake District and reintroduced birds at Rutland Water. Some of the reintroduced birds have been ringed and fitted with satellite transmitters to track their movements. The information gained from these transmitters confirmed the known pattern of migration to West Africa and provided new information on routes, speeds and stopover sites.

In July 2007, rings and satellite tags were fitted to two chicks and their mother at a nest near Forres in Scotland. The older chick drowned near the Scilly Isles on her first migratory flight and the other's transmitter failed near Malaga. However, the adult female, named Logie by pupils at the local Logie Primary School, was tracked throughout her autumn and spring migratory journeys.

Logie travelled 5,695 km to winter on the tropical island of Roxa off the coast of Guinea Bissau. The new type of solar-powered satellite tag used on Logie should last for three years and gives accurate hourly data on location, speed, direction and altitude. For example, throughout the winter Logie remained in a very small area of the island, perching mainly in one big tree in coastal woodland not far from the sea. Once or twice a day she made flights of up to a kilometre to catch fish in the South Atlantic Ocean. In the spring of 2008 Logie's return migration was again tracked on a daily basis. After several delays in bad weather, she returned to the exact tree that she set out from the previous year!

Related studies have been carried out on other raptors, such as Honey-buzzards, which have been tracked to wintering sites in West Africa. For more information about Logie and the other raptors fitted with satellite transmitters see the Highland Foundation for Wildlife website (www.roydennis.org).

THE MOVEMENTS OF 'LOGIE' THE OSPREY

The map shows the movements of 'Logie' the Osprey going south in 2007 (blue line) and returning north in 2008 (red line). Her southward migration took her a total of 5,695 km from Moray to Guinea Bissau in 55 days. Daily flights covered up to 756 km (from southern Scotland direct to France), at an average speed of 35 kph. She spent the winter on Roxa Island, favouring one big tree in an area of coastal woodland, fishing up to 1 km out into the Atlantic Ocean. Return migration was quicker, at 42 days, but was more arduous. Poor weather in northern Spain resulted in an 11-day stopover, and eventually forced her to hug the French coast rather than risk a sea crossing as she had done the previous autumn.

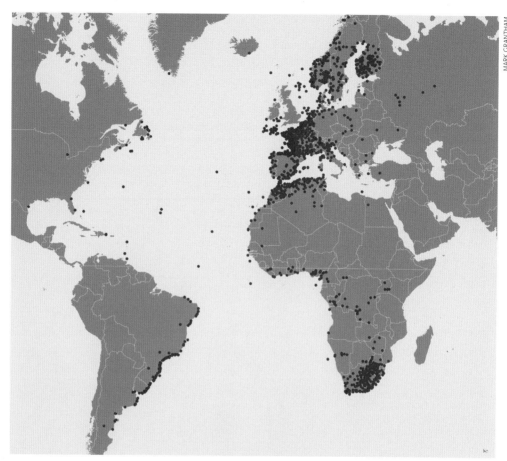

MARK GRANTHAM

Recoveries of three species of migrant that visit Britain & Ireland. Each dot represents an individual bird. Swallows (red dots) breed in Britain & Ireland and winter in southern Africa. Manx Shearwaters (brown dots) also breed here, but most cross the Atlantic for the winter. Fieldfares (blue dots) are winter visitors to Britain & Ireland, breeding well to the east.

Migratory strategies

The journey between breeding and wintering sites is often long and arduous. Without proper preparation beforehand and regular stops for food on the journey, many birds would die. The routes taken differ between species, as do the strategies. Some species make the journey in one or two long flights, while others stop off regularly to refuel. For example, ringing has shown us that Swallows fly long distances with few stops, whereas Chiffchaffs breeding in Britain & Ireland move to their wintering grounds in a series of short 'hops'. Chiffchaffs first head towards southeast England where this tiny species can take advantage of the short sea-crossing to the Continent. From early October onwards these Chiffchaffs reach the Atlantic coasts of Spain, Portugal and Morocco. Many then cross

BOX 6 UNDERSTANDING CHANGING PATTERNS OF MIGRATION

Monitoring bird movements allows us to understand why migration patterns change.

Blackcaps are more likely to pair up with partners from the same wintering area than with birds that winter elsewhere.

The pattern of migration routes is changing. Blackcaps are summer migrants to Britain, spending the winter months in southern Europe and North Africa. However, during the 1980s people began to notice that Blackcaps were also present in Britain during the winter. Initially it was thought that these were simply British birds that had not migrated, but ringing revealed a much more interesting pattern. The wintering Blackcaps are from central Europe, but instead of migrating south they migrate west. Some central European Blackcaps have always migrated west, however, harsh winters and a lack of food meant few of them survived. In recent years warmer winters and an increase in suitable food provided in gardens have greatly increased the survival rates of these birds.

Other techniques used in conjunction with ringing can help us to track and understand changing migration patterns. Stable isotope ratios in the claw tips of Blackcaps caught on their breeding grounds in Germany showed that some Blackcaps had wintered in Britain & Ireland, while others had wintered in Spain and Portugal.

Interestingly, birds were more likely to pair up with partners from the same wintering area, rather than with birds that had wintered elsewhere. Since Blackcaps that come to Britain & Ireland in winter have a shorter journey back to the central European breeding grounds, these males are able to secure the best quality territories and so these pairs rear more young. Because of this more and more Blackcaps from central Europe now migrate west to winter in Britain & Ireland.

BOX 7 EURING SWALLOW PROJECT

The European Union for Bird Ringing (EURING) Swallow Project was launched in 1997 and by 2002 nearly one million Swallows had been ringed. The project involved many hundreds of ringers in 25 different countries in Europe, Africa and Asia. This incredible effort has taught us about the lives and migration of this species.

Although it was long thought that an aerial feeder like the Swallow would not need to store fat before migration, the EURING Swallow Project showed that the amount of fat accumulation in Swallows matches that of other long-distance songbird migrants.

In addition, the Project revealed that the amount of fat stored by a Swallow when it leaves Europe to fly to Africa is related to the barriers it will have to cross before it next finds food. For example, Swallows from Italy have to cross wider stretches of the Mediterranean and the Sahara than birds from Spain. Italian Swallows thus depart with higher fat reserves than Spanish Swallows.

The amount of fat stored by Swallows depends on how far they migrate.

DAILY BODY WEIGHT CHANGES

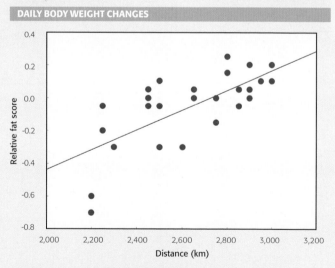

By looking at the amount of fat stored by a bird we can give it a score – the 'fat score'. The graph shows the relationship between the relative fat score of a Swallow and the size of the barriers (sea and desert) it has to cross on migration. The wider the barrier, the more fat the bird has to store to ensure it has enough fuel for the journey.

FIGURE REPRODUCED WITH KIND PERMISSION OF FERNANDO SPINA AND BLACKWELL PUBLISHING LTD.

When migrating south, Yellow Wagtails breeding in northern areas 'leap-frog' over more southerly breeding birds.

STEVE ROUND

the Sahara to occupy wintering grounds in West Africa, extending from Mauritania south to Guinea Bissau.

In some species ringing has shown us that different groups may move different distances, with those breeding the furthest north also wintering the furthest south - 'leap-frogging' over other populations of the same species. For example, Yellow Wagtails that breed in Britain and Scandinavia winter in more southerly parts of West Africa than do Yellow Wagtails that breed in the Mediterranean. The timing of spring departure from Africa also differs between these two groups, with those wintering in the northernmost areas (Mediterranean birds) departing before the rains begin, while those in more southern areas depart some weeks into the rainy season. Although birds wintering further south have a longer distance to travel, they may benefit from the increased numbers of insects in the wet season allowing them to fatten up for their long journey.

Similarly, different populations may follow different migratory routes. For example, Common Terns breeding in western Europe migrate down the western coasts of Europe and Africa, with the majority wintering along the west coast of Africa, although some birds (particularly those from Fennoscandia) winter in southern Africa. In contrast, Common Terns breeding in eastern Europe migrate through the eastern Mediterranean and Red Sea to winter on the east coast of Africa.

Weighing and measuring birds when we catch them for ringing has shown us how they prepare themselves for migration by building up reserves of fat and muscle to fuel their journey. Different species prepare for migratory journeys in different ways. Some birds put on a lot of fat before undertaking long flights, while others stop more frequently on their journey and therefore do not require large fat stores. Box 7 (page 30) gives an example of birds that store different amounts of fat depending on the distance they need to travel.

Some species, particularly warblers, also change their diet, switching from insects to sugar-rich fruit in the pre-migration period, allowing them to fatten up quickly. This will provide them with fuel during their journey. A study of fat stores and organ sizes of Bar-tailed Godwits that died after hitting a radar dome on the Alaska Peninsula showed that most had large amounts of fat but comparatively small gizzards, livers, kidneys and guts. This suggests that prior to departure at least some long-distance migrants are able to reduce the size of body organs that are not directly necessary for flight, minimising their overall body weight and allowing them to fly more efficiently. Once they arrive at their destination the birds build up their organs back to normal size.

Stopover sites

Stopover sites are places where birds stop off to rest and feed during their journey. Such sites are often located before geographical barriers such as oceans, deserts, or mountain ranges. The length of time a bird spends at a stopover site depends on its condition (especially the amount of fat it has) and how far it has to go before refuelling again, as well as the weather, wind direction and the quality of the stopover habitat. Stopover sites are critical for the survival of a bird on its long journey. If a bird is unable to feed up along the way it may arrive on its breeding grounds late or in poor condition and have a poor breeding season; worse still, it may die on the journey. By catching and weighing birds at stopover sites we are able to compare their condition between years and determine if any changes to the site (eg increased human activity) are changing the quality and value of the site for the birds.

PARTIAL AND DIFFERENTIAL MIGRATION

When some individuals in a population migrate but others do not, this is called partial migration. We are not sure exactly why this happens but it probably depends on a range of factors, such as the genetic make-up of an individual, environmental conditions and where a bird fits in the 'pecking order'. In cases where some individuals migrate every year, partial migration is likely to be controlled genetically. In other cases, partial migration may occur only in some years as a response to weather or food availability. Ringing can help us to understand partial migration, for example, it has shown that few of the Blackbirds that breed in Britain & Ireland migrate, while those from more northerly parts of Europe generally migrate south for the winter.

TOMMY HOLDEN/JOHN HARDING

Above left: Ringing has shown us that female Ruff ringed in Britain tend to winter in Africa, while the males tend to winter in Europe. Above right: The scientific species name of the Chaffinch *coelebs* is from the Latin word for bachelor. This is because the females winter further south than the males, so wintering flocks in northern Europe often consist mainly of males.

Partial migration is essentially a trade-off:

- Migrating individuals: avoid food shortages in the winter but risk a long and potentially dangerous journey.

- Resident individuals: risk starvation but will be the first birds on the breeding site the following season. This may allow resident birds to get the best territories and start breeding earlier.

Sometimes individuals of different ages or sexes breed in the same area but winter in different places. This is known as differential migration. Ringing can help us to identify the strategies used by different groups of birds. For example, female Ruff ringed in Britain tend to winter in Africa, while the males tend to winter in Europe. As with partial migration, the most suitable wintering area is a trade-off between remaining close to the breeding site or surviving the winter by moving greater distances to find food. Staying close to the breeding site may be more important for males than females, as this allows the males to pick the best breeding territories before the females arrive. In fact, this is how the Chaffinch got its scientific species name: *coelebs* from the Latin word for bachelor, reflecting the fact that flocks wintering in Sweden are mostly males because the females winter further south. For females, avoiding starvation may be the top priority. If they do not find enough food during the winter, they may be in poor condition the following spring, which will affect their breeding performance, or they may even die.

Where there is a difference between age groups (*eg* Lapwing), ringing has shown us that immature birds tend to migrate further than adults.

STEVE ROUND

This may be because immature birds tend to be smaller than the more dominant adults and so are less able to compete for limited food resources. For young birds the only chance of survival may be to travel longer distances to find food.

COLD WEATHER MOVEMENTS

Cold weather is not such a big problem for birds as we might imagine, as they are equipped with two good survival tools: insulating feathers and the ability to fly. However, they need to find and eat enough food to build and maintain fat supplies to see them through harsh weather. Some species respond to cold weather by moving and the sight of flocks of Lapwing and Golden Plover flying to the milder south and southwest in search of ice-free feeding areas tells us it is really cold. In particularly cold weather there are increased reports in France and Iberia of Lapwing ringed in Britain & Ireland. Other species respond by changing their behaviour – by feeding more intensively or for longer.

Some birds make altitudinal movements within Britain to escape harsh winter weather. For example, Ptarmigans move lower down the mountain slopes and Yellowhammers move from upland breeding areas to lower altitudes for shelter and food.

Above: The sight of flocks of Lapwing flying to the milder south and southwest in search of ice-free feeding areas tells us it is really cold!
Right: Ptarmigans breed on high mountain tops, but in winter move to lower altitudes to find food.

EDMUND FELLOWES

JANE AND MIKE MALPASS

IRRUPTIONS

From time to time both Britain and Ireland receive influxes of birds from abroad in search of food. The most familiar of these is the Waxwing, which can occur in huge numbers in some winters. Their arrival in Britain usually coincides with a successful breeding season and a crash in the local food supply, particularly their favourite Rowan berries. This kind of movement is known as an irruption. Other species that move in response to a lack of food include Siskin, Brambling and Crossbill.

We know a lot about the movements of Waxwings within Britain thanks to volunteer ringers who have concentrated on catching them and fitting colour rings. Because they are often seen in gardens, town and cities, members of the public and birdwatchers are able to read the combination of colour rings and report the sightings. Colour-ringing has revealed some spectacular movements of birds within Britain, showing how they move south during the winter in search of food. They will devour all the berries in an area and then move on in search of more food.

Waxwings can occur in huge numbers in some winters. The arrival of these birds in Britain usually coincides with a food shortage in their normal range. The colour rings on this bird enable it to be identified as an individual without being recaught.

MOULT MIGRATION

While songbirds replace wing feathers one after another (Box 4, page 23) some groups of birds, particularly wildfowl and seabirds, moult all of

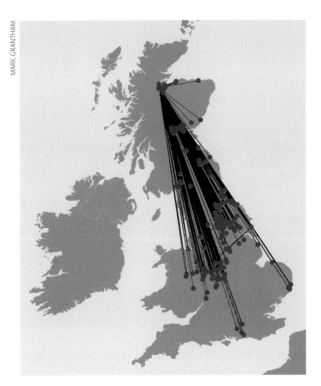

MARK GRANTHAM

Canada Geese gathering to moult their flight feathers on the Beauly Firth originate from all over Britain. The map shows movements of individual ringed birds. The blue dots represent birds that have been shot or found dead, while the red dots are birds that have been resighted or retrapped.

their wing feathers at the same time and become flightless until they grow new feathers. This makes them vulnerable to predation so many of these species move to a safe site to moult, usually somewhere that is close to, or surrounded by, a large area of water. For example, ringing has shown us that many of the Shelduck that breed in Europe moult in the Helgoland Bight off the north coast of Germany. To reach the Bight Shelduck from different breeding areas travel in very different directions, with those from Britain flying east or southeast, while those from southern France fly north. Ringing has also shown us that Canada Geese introduced into Britain have established a moult migration to the Beauly Firth in Scotland. This mirrors the moult migrations of Canada Geese in their native North America.

DISPERSAL

Following the breeding season, young birds move away from the area in which they hatched (their natal area) and disperse into the surrounding region, exploring it in search of food. Ringing has shown us that many birds return to the natal area to breed in subsequent years, although in some species one sex may disperse further than the other to reduce the risk of inbreeding. Despite migrating to Africa for the winter, most of our warblers return to breed within 15-20 km of where they were hatched.

STUART SHARP

Cetti's Warblers colonised southeast England in the 1960s and 1970s. The species has benefitted from the recent mild winters and the population continues to expand and spread inland.

The young of resident species also disperse but tend not to move far from the area where they hatched. Barn Owls usually move less than 10 km and smaller species, such as Blue Tits, usually breed within a kilometre of the nest they were raised in.

Most birds return to the same breeding area each year. When birds change their breeding areas this is called breeding dispersal. Breeding dispersal may be a response to a poor breeding season. Alternatively, if many birds breed successfully in a particular area, afterwards some birds disperse away from their breeding site. These birds may then stay and breed in new areas. For example, the number of Little Egrets in Britain & Ireland has increased dramatically in recent years. These birds are thought to have dispersed from breeding sites in France where the numbers of birds that breed successfully has recently increased. Ringing will help us to understand these changing patterns in dispersal.

Another species that has recently colonised Britain is Cetti's Warbler. The first record of a Cetti's Warbler in Britain was in 1961 and numbers began to increase in the early 1970s. The population has expanded into East Anglia and south Wales, and spread inland. Analysis of ringing data shows that this was mainly due to dispersal of young birds. As the available habitats in the area that was originally colonised filled up, young birds had to disperse further to find suitable places to breed.

CHAPTER 04

Bird Ringing as a Tool for Monitoring and Conservation

Although bird ringing started as a way of finding out about the movements of birds, today it also helps us to monitor numbers of birds from year to year, as well as investigating their breeding success and survival. This is particularly important at a time when humans are having an increasing impact on the environment and many bird populations are under threat from factors such as changes in agriculture, climate change and oil spills. It is likely that the importance of ringing will continue to grow as we try to understand the consequences of our actions.

Ringers are encouraged to focus on particular species or groups of birds that are of conservation concern, but we also encourage the ringing of a wide range of species, as we don't know where the conservation interests of the future may lie. House Sparrows are extremely sedentary and in the 1960s and 1970s they were so common that they were not thought interesting enough to ring. Yet when the population began to decline

JOHN HARDING

in the 1990s, had they been ringed, this information would have been invaluable to help us to understand why numbers were falling.

This chapter looks in more detail at how ringing is used to monitor bird populations and to understand the cause of population declines, showing why ringing is a vital tool for conservation.

BRINGING INFORMATION TOGETHER

The Ringing Scheme forms a major part of the BTO's Integrated Population Monitoring (IPM) programme: by combining the results of ringing with those from other schemes we can get a much fuller picture of how and why populations change. Schemes such as the Breeding Bird Survey and Wetland Bird Survey focus on monitoring changes in numbers between years. The Nest Record Scheme looks at the breeding success of species by recording the contents of a nest and making repeat visits to record the success or failure of that nest (Box 1, page 14). The BTO also organises specific ringing projects, such as the Constant Effort Sites Scheme and the Retrapping Adults for Survival Scheme to gain extra information on adult survival and productivity.

When we notice an increase or decline in a population we can bring together the results of these various surveys to investigate which part of the birds' life cycle has been affected and may have led to the change in the population.

House Sparrows were once thought too common to ring but the population began to decline in the 1980s. Ringing is an important bird monitoring tool, allowing us to understand when and why changes in populations occur.

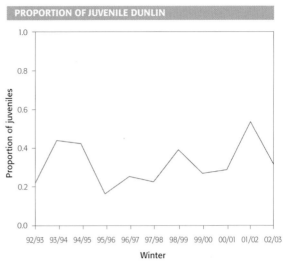

The proportion of juveniles in catches of waders in the winter gives us a measure of breeding success. This example shows the proportion of juvenile Dunlin caught in Britain & Ireland in the winter in different years.

MEASURING BREEDING SUCCESS

Most of the information we have about breeding success comes from CES ringing and the Nest Record Scheme, which records laying dates, clutch sizes and how many chicks survive to fledge from the nest. However, some birds that spend the winter in Britain breed hundreds of miles away in inhospitable landscapes, where monitoring breeding success is difficult. For example, many of our wintering waders breed in the arctic tundra. For these species calculating the proportion of young birds caught by ringers in Britain & Ireland each year can give us an indication of annual breeding success.

SURVIVAL STUDIES

Once birds have reached adulthood, many species remain faithful to a particular area, especially during the breeding season. Remarkably, many of our summer visitors from Africa return to exactly the same area in which they bred the previous year. Extracting a migrant warbler from a mist net in the spring, finding that it already has a ring from a previous year, and knowing that it has been to Africa and back in the meantime, is a humbling experience. Even more remarkable is discovering that the bird was previously caught in exactly the same net! Because many species return to the same breeding area we can catch them year after year, and find out how many birds have survived from one year to the next.

STEVE ROUND

RETRAPPING ADULTS FOR SURVIVAL

Changes in the number of birds that survive from year to year have caused population changes in many species. General ringing gives us good information on survival, but we can learn even more about a population by carrying out targeted studies. The Retrapping Adults for Survival (RAS) Scheme encourages ringers to target particular species that we know little about. RAS ringers choose a species and study area where they aim to recatch or resight at least 30 adult birds per year. RAS projects focus on species that are not well-monitored by general or Constant Effort ringing, such as Pied Flycatcher or House Sparrow.

There are a number of RAS studies on Swallows, House Martins and Sand Martins. For these species we have found that the number of adult birds surviving from one year to the next is related to rainfall on the African wintering grounds. This is probably because the rainfall allows plants to flourish and numbers of insects, which the birds feed on, to increase. In wetter years there are more insects and more birds survive. As the global climate changes, it is important to know how conditions in different parts of the species' breeding and wintering areas affect survival, so that if the population changes, we can understand why.

Many of the migrant birds that we catch in Britain & Ireland in the spring, such as this Grasshopper Warbler, have flown all the way to Africa and back! Around a third of adults make it back each year.

JOHN HARDING

Information from ringing and nest records helps us to understand why populations of some birds, such as the Lapwing, are declining.

RINGING AS A TOOL FOR UNDERSTANDING POPULATION DECLINES

Why Have Farmland Birds Declined?

The jangling sound of the Corn Bunting's song or the 'pee-wit' call of the Lapwing as they tumbled over fields in the spring were once familiar over much of Britain. However, since the late 1970s populations of many farmland birds have declined, some by as much as half. Information from the Ringing and Nest Record Schemes has helped us understand the reasons for these declines.

Analysis of reports of ringed birds found dead show that, for many species, the number of young birds surviving the winter appears to be lower, particularly during cold winters (see graph overleaf for Song Thrush). This is because young birds are less efficient at finding food, and tend to be excluded from the best sites by the competitively superior adults. More efficient harvesting, stronger herbicides and drainage of fields all mean that there is not as much good quality habitat for birds to forage in, so mortality rates, especially of young birds, increase.

For Lapwing, there appears to be no change in mortality rates from analysis of the ringing data, but data from nest records show that fewer young birds are being produced each year. Again, this reduction in

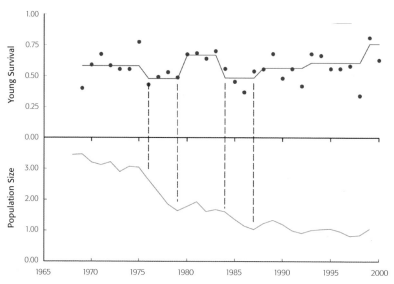

SURVIVAL OF YOUNG SONG THRUSHES AND POPULATION SIZE

The proportion of young Song Thrushes surviving varies between years (top graph, dots). During periods when relatively few survive (top graph, line), the population tends to decline (bottom graph). Note the steepness of the decline in the periods marked by the dashed lines (1976-79 and 1984-87).

breeding success is probably the result of changes in agricultural practice. Lapwings need different habitat types during the breeding season: open ground for nesting and grassland for their chicks to find food safely. With the demise of mixed farming in many parts of the country, such crop diversity is becoming harder for Lapwings to find so fewer are raising successful broods.

Armed with this knowledge of why populations have changed, we have worked closely with government and others to design options within agri-environment schemes that farmers can use to increase the number of birds on their farms. For example, farmers are encouraged to include fallow plots for breeding Lapwings, areas of food rich habitat for seed-eating birds and damp habitat for Song Thrushes. Knowing the reasons for the declines means we can be confident that these options should have a real impact on the numbers of birds.

Starlings and House Sparrows – Pest Species?

The Starling and House Sparrow are almost ubiquitous in Britain. Indeed, they have usually been thought of as pest species, particularly by farmers, because large flocks would descend on newly harvested grain stacks, and by public health officials worried about fouling of pavements. As a consequence, both species were covered by a general licence allowing for their control where they posed an economic or public health threat. However, numbers have declined to such an extent in the last thirty

JOHN HARDING

The number of Starlings in Britain has declined so dramatically that their status has changed from that of a pest, to a species of high conservation concern.

years that they are now placed on the 'Red List' of species of highest conservation concern.

Ringing has shown that the population decline of Starlings has largely been caused by lowered survival of young birds, while that of House Sparrows is a result of a number of factors. As with farmland birds, food supplies in the wider countryside are becoming scarcer for Starlings, so they are coming into gardens in much greater numbers during cold winters than they were previously. The results of our analyses of ringing and other data demonstrated that Starling and House Sparrow populations were under pressure, and so both species have been removed from the list of those that may be controlled under general licences.

Protecting estuarine habitat

Ringing can provide detailed information on habitat use, which can provide important information for conservation purposes. A good example of this is a detailed study in Cardiff Bay before and after the mudflats were enclosed by a barrage, converting them into a freshwater lagoon, as part of an urban regeneration programme. The mudflats provided foraging habitat

Ringing studies have shown that the number of Oystercatchers that survive from year to year is closely linked to how cold the weather is and how many shellfish are available for the birds to eat.

during the winter for a number of species, including Redshank, many of which were marked with metal and colour rings. Redshank are normally very faithful to a particular wintering site but, following the impoundment of the mudflats, many of the Redshank which had previously used the Bay were forced to move to the neighbouring Rhymney mudflats.

The birds displaced from Cardiff Bay, however, were unable to forage effectively in their new home and their mortality rate increased by 44% in the three years following the closure of the barrage. Birds that had always spent the winter at Rhymney showed no decline in survival rates over the same period. Having to move wintering site lowered survival rate, perhaps because the birds that had to move were excluded from the best sites by the existing occupants, or they simply did not know the best areas to forage in, rather than because they had moved to a poorer quality site.

Knowledge of the movements of marked birds was equally important in evaluating the impacts of a proposal to build a new container port in Dibden Bay on the Solent. This proposal was eventually rejected because of the conservation importance of the site. Our estuaries face ever increasing pressures from developers wishing to use them for a wide variety of purposes. One proposed solution where sites are of conservation importance is that alternative habitat could be created close by, as was suggested at Dibden. The results of the Cardiff Bay study show that such proposals need to be considered carefully as the long-term impacts on the birds may not be immediately obvious.

Shellfish Management and Oystercatchers

Ringing studies on the Wash in Norfolk and Lincolnshire have shown that the number of Oystercatchers that survive from year to year is closely linked to how cold the weather is and how many Cockles and Mussels are available for the birds to eat. When there is cold weather, or a shortage of either Cockles or Mussels, the number of adults that survive from one year to the next falls, but only slightly. However, when there is a shortage of both Cockles and Mussels, survival drops markedly because there is no good alternative food source.

Ringing has shown that if Oystercatchers do not have enough food in the autumn, they stop moulting their feathers and keep some of the old ones. This is bad news for an Oystercatcher because its feathers will be old and worn. It takes a lot of energy to moult and grow new feathers and a bird will only stop moulting if it is not getting enough food. Finding that Oystercatchers have not completed their moult in autumn gives us an early warning that they are finding things hard and that higher numbers than usual are likely to die in the winter.

DAWN BALMER

The Constant Effort Sites Scheme is a programme of standardised mist-netting in scrub, woodland, or reedbed sites like this one.

CONSTANT EFFORT SITES

General ringing can tell us much about long-term changes in bird populations but we can improve annual monitoring if each year we put up the same nets, in the same place and for the same length of time. To do this we run the Constant Effort Sites (CES) Scheme during the breeding season (May to August) in scrub, reedbed and woodland habitats. Keeping our catching effort constant from year to year like this allows us to compare changes in numbers of birds present, how many juveniles are produced and how well birds survive.

What can it tell us?

■ Numbers of birds

Because CES uses a standardised approach we can use changes in the number of adults caught between years to monitor the ups and downs in numbers. Species such as Reed Warbler and Sedge Warbler specialise in reedbed habitats making them difficult to measure using standard counting methods. CES ringing is a very effective way to monitor numbers of these elusive birds.

■ Survival

By looking at the number of ringed birds that return to CE sites we can work out how many birds survive each year. Using information

STEVE ROUND

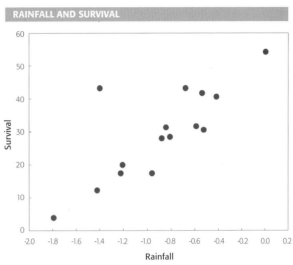

RAINFALL AND SURVIVAL

Many migrant species, such as Sedge Warbler, migrate through the Sahel in West Africa. In years with high rainfall food for Sedge Warblers (mostly insects) is more plentiful. In years of low rainfall there is not enough food, so many birds do not survive.

from CE Sites, for example, we have been able to relate the number of adult Sedge Warblers that survive each year to rainfall in West Africa. In winters when rainfall is high in West Africa the number of Sedge Warblers surviving from year to year goes up.

▨ Breeding success
By looking at the number of young birds caught in comparison to the number of adults we can get a good idea of breeding success each year. The breeding success of around 25 species is measured by CES ringing. Breeding success in any year is often linked to short-term weather events. For example, in dry summers the breeding success of Blackbirds and Song Thrushes is low as the hard ground means that the adults cannot get enough worms to feed their young. Box 8 (page 50) shows how CES helps us to understand population change.

European collaboration
Over 15 CES Schemes operate across Europe using methods very similar to those developed in Britain & Ireland. This gives us an opportunity to look at numbers of common species across many countries. The patterns we see in different countries are quite similar, particularly for breeding success. This suggests that environmental factors that influence breeding success can affect birds across an entire continent.

BOX 8 UNDERSTANDING THE DECLINE IN NUMBERS OF WILLOW WARBLERS

Ringing will help us to understand why Willow Warblers are declining in some areas.

The Willow Warbler is a common summer visitor to Britain & Ireland but over the last 25 years the population has declined by over 50%.

Willow Warbler numbers have not declined over the whole of Britain & Ireland. There are now fewer Willow Warblers in southern Britain, but Scottish populations have remained stable. Analysis of CES data has shown that the number of adults surviving from year to year fell in the south in the early 1990s, although there was no change in the north.

The reason why fewer birds are surviving is not known, but it may be that birds from northern Britain winter in different parts of Africa than those from the south and that birds from the south are faced with more problems on the wintering grounds. The BTO is working with researchers at the University of East Anglia to understand why Willow Warblers are declining.

The Willow Warbler is a common summer visitor to Britain and Ireland but over the last 25 years the population has declined by over 50%.

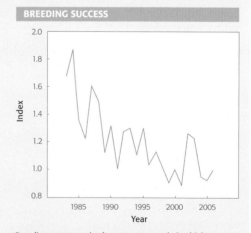

The numbers of adult Willow Warblers caught on CE sites has declined since the start of CES ringing in 1983.

Breeding success varies from year to year, being higher when the weather is good, as parents find it easier to collect food for their chicks, and lower in poor weather. Overall there is a long-term decline.

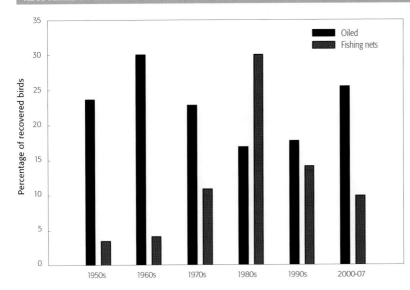

RECOVERIES OF GUILLEMOTS THAT ARE OILED OR CAUGHT IN FISHING NETS

Oiled
Fishing nets

Percentage of recovered birds

1950s 1960s 1970s 1980s 1990s 2000-07

Seabirds are vulnerable to human activities. Around 20% of all ringed Guillemots that are reported to us are found oiled (black bars) and up to 30% are found in fishing nets (blue bars).

CONSERVATION ISSUES

Human impacts on seabirds

Britain & Ireland is home to around 4 million pairs of seabirds and holds internationally important numbers of several species. During the breeding season the birds are found largely on inaccessible cliffs and islands, spending the rest of the year at sea. While at sea they are vulnerable to human activities. For example, large numbers of ringed Guillemots reported dead are killed by oil or fishing nets. The change from woven nets, easily avoided by seabirds, to almost invisible monofilament nets in the 1960s meant that many more Guillemots died in fishing nets. A ban on monofilament nets in the late 1980s and a general reduction in fishing effort may have been responsible for the decrease in casualties from fishing nets in recent years.

Ringing has shown us that seabirds from different colonies around Britain & Ireland tend to winter in different sea areas. In some species birds of different ages also winter in different areas. For example, Guillemots breeding along the east coast of Britain will spend the winter in the North Sea (as adults) or off the coast of Norway (as juveniles), whereas those breeding along the west coast of Britain and in Ireland will winter as far south as the Bay of Biscay. Ringing of these seabirds in breeding colonies not only gives us information on where they winter, but can also help us to predict the likely effect of incidents at sea, such as a major oil spill. For example, the *Prestige* oil spill in northwest Spain on

JAN VAN FRANEKER

13 November 2002 affected mostly Guillemots from colonies in Ireland and Wales, while the oil spill that resulted from the sinking of the *Tricolor* off the coast of Belgium on 14 December 2002 affected mainly Guillemots breeding along the Scottish east coast. Understanding the age and origin of seabirds affected by oiling is vital to assess the real impact of oil on populations of these birds.

Using ringing data we have also found that oil spills not only cause direct problems for seabirds (by damaging their feathers, and being swallowed), they can have longer-term effects - fewer Guillemots survive during the winter when there has been an oil spill. This is because the oil kills the fish that seabirds feed on.

Recoveries of dead seabirds show how they are affected by human impacts such as oil spills.

Hunting

Reports of ringed birds found dead tell us about the main causes of mortality. We rely on members of the public to report birds they find with rings on and these records can be subsequently used in analyses, often together with records from other ringing schemes across Europe.

For example, Woodcock are legal quarry in most parts of Europe and are hunted regularly. In autumn large numbers of Woodcocks move into France, Britain and the Low Countries to escape the harsh winters further north. We can investigate the pressure of hunting in Europe by looking at reports of ringed birds that have died from hunting or other causes.

Species such as Woodcock are legal quarry in most parts of Europe. Information from ringing allows us to monitor the effects of hunting on populations.

HERBERT & HOWELLS

Timing of breeding and migration

Ringing and Nest Record data can be used to monitor the timing of breeding in birds. This can help us to understand environmental impacts, from small-scale effects such as habitat management, to global-scale factors such as climate change. For example, a study on moorland bird species showed that controlled burning of vegetation at the wrong time of year could affect the breeding success of birds.

Burning is a traditional method for encouraging the growth of new shoots and plants, which grouse feed on. Although burning has to be carried out within a certain time period (between autumn and spring), it may still be a problem for birds, particularly those that nest early in the season, such as Oystercatcher and Peregrine. The study showed that burning could also affect Hen Harrier, Stonechat and possibly Ring Ouzel. Not only can burning destroy nests, it can also destroy the insects and other animals that moorland birds feed on. Since the 1970s, a wide range of British & Irish breeding species have started breeding earlier in the season as our climate has changed. If moorland birds are breeding earlier they may become even more vulnerable to the effects of burning.

MONITORING DISEASE

Ringing can help us to understand the development and spread of disease in birds, such as Avian Influenza (AI). In 1996 a highly pathogenic strain of AI evolved in southeast Asia, eventually spreading to Europe. AI can

STEVE ROUND

potentially be spread in a number of ways, including the transport of domestic poultry or poultry products, movement of poultry workers, the cage bird trade and the movement of wild birds. Understanding the likely risk of wild birds spreading AI is very important.

To look at the potential risk of AI being moved across Europe by migrating wild birds, the BTO worked with other European ringing schemes to analyse information on wild bird movements based on ringing data. By combining information about the direction, distance and timing of each bird movement, a European 'migration mapping tool' was developed (www.euring.org/ai-eu). The mapping shows us when different species migrate and where they are moving from and to. This means that if there is an outbreak of AI in a given area we can predict the likelihood of AI being moved by a particular species. For example, an outbreak of AI in France during the breeding season is unlikely to be brought into Britain & Ireland by Wigeon, but an outbreak in the Low Countries or Germany during the breeding season would be of far greater concern (see map on page 56).

Although the mapping tool was developed to look at the risks of AI spreading through Europe, the same techniques are also useful for understanding the movements of other migratory birds.

Birds breeding on moorland such as Stonechats (above) and Peregrines (right) that nest early in the breeding season may be vulnerable to the effects of burning of vegetation.

HOWARD PATON

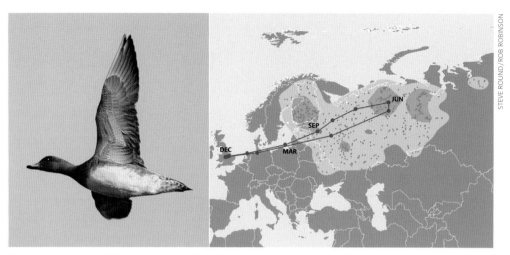

STEVE ROUND/ROB ROBINSON

Migratory movements of Wigeon wintering in Britain. The shaded areas show where most of our recoveries occur (pink shading 50% of recoveries, blue shading 95% of recoveries, actual recoveries grey dots). The large red dots connected by lines show the average location of birds each month.

SUMMARY

During the hundred years of organised ringing in Britain & Ireland we have gathered a vast amount of information about many species of birds. The original aim of the Ringing Scheme was to understand where birds migrated to and why, and we now understand a great deal about their movements. However, in the last twenty years the value of ringing for conservation purposes has become evident.

The examples in this chapter show how ringing has allowed us to identify changes in the patterns of bird movements and populations, as well as some of the causes underlying them. As the global human population grows and our climate changes, pressures on the environment at home and abroad are bound to increase. Through a combination of targeted projects and more general ringing we can gather information that could not be obtained in any other way to inform conservation policy. Increasingly, the threats that bird populations face are international in scope. By its very nature ringing encourages collaboration across countries, helping to develop co-ordinated responses to these problems.

Ringing is now an integral tool in monitoring our bird populations and we will continue to develop ringing as a tool for conservation over the next 100 years. Everyone who rings a bird, or finds one and reports it to the BTO should do so knowing that they are directly contributing to our knowledge about, and conservation of, Britain & Ireland's bird populations.

CHAPTER 05

Getting Involved

This chapter describes the different ways you can contribute to our work, including what to do if you see a bird with a ring on and how you can become a ringer yourself. It also explains what the BTO does and how you can get involved in other surveys that we carry out.

HOW TO REPORT A RINGED BIRD

If you find a dead bird with a ring on, or see a bird with colour marks (rings, wing tags, neck collars *etc*), you can help our research by sending the details to the Ringing Scheme at BTO HQ. All BTO rings fitted to wild birds have an address on them. The address on BTO rings is that of the Natural History Museum, which was chosen because it is easily recognised by finders around the world. Some rings also have a website address. Details of any ring, including those with foreign scheme addresses, can be reported directly to BTO HQ using the details overleaf.

Report your ring to:

Online: www.ring.ac

By mail: The Ringing Unit
BTO, The Nunnery, Thetford, Norfolk IP24 2PU

By telephone: 01842 750050

By Email: ringing@bto.org

Either fill in the website form or, if writing or emailing, please give us the following information:

Species:
Tell us the species if you know it.
Ring number or exact position of colour marks:
Write down the ring number and if the bird is dead, please carefully tape the ring (flattened) to your letter if writing, otherwise please keep it in a safe place. Let us know if you would like to have the ring back and we will return it to you. If it is not a BTO ring (address starting BTO, British Museum or NH Museum) please also give the address, as it may have been ringed abroad. For colour-marked birds note the exact position of the metal ring and colour marks (*eg* left or right leg, above or below the 'knee') and include details of any inscription on the colour marks.
Where:
Give the location where the bird was found including the name of the nearest town or village, county and a grid reference if possible.
When:
Give the date the ringed bird was found or seen.
Circumstances:
Tell us whether the bird was alive or dead. If dead please give the cause of death if known, *eg* was it hit by a car, brought in by a cat, or found oiled on a beach? Also note if the bird was freshly dead or decomposed *etc*. If the bird is alive, please say what happened to it. If you used binoculars or a telescope to read colour marks please say so.
Your details:
Don't forget to give your name, address and email so that we can send you the information about when and where the bird was ringed. Details will normally be sent within six weeks, but there may be delays at busy times of year. If you send a report of a ringed bird by email, please include your postal address.

DAWN BALMER

All ringers in Britain & Ireland are trained to a very high standard to ensure that birds are caught and handled safely and efficiently.

Rings from other sources

Sometimes birds are found with rings that have not been put on by a ringing scheme, for example, racing pigeons or escaped cage birds. Details of how to report these rings are available on the BTO website (www.ring.ac).

HOW TO BECOME A RINGER

All ringers in Britain & Ireland are trained to a very high standard to ensure that birds are handled safely and efficiently. The skills that you need to become a ringer are learnt by practice, under the close supervision of experienced ringers. Potential trainees work with an experienced trainer, who teaches them all the necessary skills to catch, handle and age birds. By ringing regularly throughout the year a trainee will see birds of different ages and at different stages of moult and will learn how features such as feather shape and wear can help to age birds. When the trainer is satisfied that a high standard of ringing has been

LUKE DELVE

All reports of ringed birds are useful for our research. Left: a colour-marked Puffin, above: a dead Shag wearing a ring.

reached, the trainee will be given a provisional or 'C' permit allowing them to ring without the direct guidance of the trainer. For most trainee ringers who want to ring a variety of species, this initial phase of training will take about two years, but this varies depending on the aptitude of the trainee and how frequently they are able to ring.

Further ringing and training may lead to a full or 'A' permit and complete independence from a trainer. Some 'A' permit holders with the necessary skills become trainers themselves and so the scheme evolves. If you are interested in becoming a ringer the first step is to visit our website (www.bto.org/goto/train2ring.htm) to find out who rings locally to you. You will then be able to go out ringing a few times to get an idea of what is involved – early mornings are not for everyone!

For some projects a ringer may not need to have experience and knowledge of all aspects of ringing so they can train for a licence specific to their needs. Depending on the nature of the study it may take as little as a few weeks to gain the experience required, for example to ring chicks of one species, or to ring adult Mute Swans. Any study involving the use of a mist net will take longer as mist nets are not selective in the species they catch.

FURTHER INFORMATION

Ringing

If you would like more information about bird ringing, or are interested in training to become a bird ringer, please visit the BTO ringers' webpages for more details (www.bto.org/ringing).

The BTO

The BTO is a registered charity, with an HQ in Thetford, Norfolk and a Scottish office based at the University of Stirling. The BTO's main objectives are to promote and encourage the wider understanding, appreciation and conservation of birds. Much of the work carried out by the BTO relies on volunteers who carry out field surveys, including:

■ The **Nest Record Scheme** gathers information on the breeding success of our birds See Box 1, page 14 for more information, or the NRS website (www.bto.org/survey/nest_records).

■ **Garden BirdWatch** is a simple weekly survey of the bird species using a volunteer's garden. Gardens are an important habitat for many wild birds and this survey allows us to gather important information on how different species of birds use gardens and how this use changes over time (www.bto.org/gbw).

■ **BirdTrack** is a free online bird recording system, increasing the value of your birdwatching records personally, locally and nationally. By simply collating lists of birds, the survey tracks the pattern and timing of bird movements and adds to our knowledge of bird distributions, directly contributing to conservation action. To register, visit the BirdTrack website (www.bto.org/birdtrack).

■ The **Breeding Bird Survey** is a national project aimed at keeping track of changes in the breeding populations of widespread bird species in the UK. The status of wild bird populations is an important indicator of the health of the countryside. During each breeding season, volunteers make three visits to an allocated 1 km square to record the birds they see and hear (www.bto.org/bbs).

■ The **Wetland Bird Survey** is a scheme that monitors non-breeding waterbirds, providing important information for the conservation of their populations and wetland habitats. Co-ordinated counts are made, mostly by volunteers, throughout the year with a focus on the winter months and passage periods (www.bto.org/webs).

Ringing often involves a lot of teamwork. Ringers come from all walks of life and there is always something new that can be learned by working closely with others.

The results from BTO monitoring studies (updated annually) are available online (www.bto.org/survey). To find out more about the BTO, including how to become a member, or how you can take part in one of our volunteer surveys, please visit our website (www.bto.org), or contact BTO HQ (see back cover).

Further Reading

There are many useful books and publications available from the BTO or good bookshops, including the ones listed below. For information about these, including how to order them, visit the BTO website (www.bto.org/membership/sales.htm).

- Elphick, J. (ed) (2007) *Natural History Museum Atlas of Bird Migration.* The Natural History Museum, London.
- EURING (2007) *Bird Ringing for Science and Conservation.* This booklet is available to download as a pdf file: www.euring.org/about_euring/brochure2007/euring_brochure_2007.pdf
- Newton, I. (2007) *The Migration Ecology of Birds.* Academic Press, London.
- Flegg, J. (2004) *Time to Fly: exploring bird migration.* BTO, Thetford.
- Wernham, C.V., Toms, M.P., Marchant, J.H., Clark, J.A., Siriwardena, G.M. and Baillie, S.R. (eds) (2002) *The Migration Atlas: movements of the birds of Britain and Ireland.* T. & A.D. Poyser, London.

CHAPTER 06

Frequently Asked Questions & Record Breakers

This chapter aims to answer many of the questions we are asked most often, such as how many birds are ringed each year and when scientific ringing started. It also includes information about record-breaking birds, including the longest-lived species and those that travel the furthest.

FREQUENTLY ASKED QUESTIONS

Does ringing affect birds?

The simple answer is no. It is essential that birds are not affected unduly by the fitting and wearing of a ring; if they were, ringing would not be telling us how normal birds behave. Many studies have shown that ringed birds quickly return to feeding, roosting, incubating eggs or feeding chicks once they are released and long distance migrants continue to travel thousands of miles between breeding and wintering grounds. Any effect is kept to a minimum as ringing is carried out by skilled ringers with the utmost consideration for the birds' welfare.

How heavy are rings?

Rings vary in weight depending on the species they are designed for. A ring for a Long-tailed Tit or Wren weighs just 0.04 g and the average weight for these species is around 9 g. This means the ring weighs just 0.4% of the bird's body weight. A ring designed to fit birds the size of a Blackbird weighs around 0.14 g, which is only around 0.1% of the bird's body weight. The biggest rings, designed to fit species such as Mute Swan, weigh around 4.3 g – a mere 0.04% of the bird's body weight.

How do you catch birds?

Birds are caught in a variety of ways. Some birds are ringed as chicks in the nest so their precise age and origin are known. Most songbirds are caught using mist nets. These are very fine, but strong, nets that are stretched out between tall poles and are difficult to see. They have a series of 'shelves' built into the netting so that when a bird flies into the net it falls into a 'pocket' and can be extracted safely. Where conditions are unsuitable for mist nets (eg coastal bird observatories) a Helgoland trap can be used. This is effectively a large funnel built out of wire and wood, which directs birds into a catching box at the end. Flocking species, such as geese, waders and gulls, are often caught with whoosh nets (named after the noise they make) and cannon nets (a bigger version of the whoosh net). For more information see Chapter 2.

How long does it take to train as a ringer?

How long it takes to train to become a ringer depends on how often you are able to go out ringing and what kind of ringing permit you want to achieve. The necessary skills can only be learnt by practice under the close supervision of experienced ringers. Essential skills include the safe and efficient trapping and handling of birds, species identification, ageing, sexing, measuring and record keeping. For this reason, ringers generally train for at least one or two years during which they are only allowed to ring birds under supervision. However, if you are looking for a restricted permit, for example to ring chicks of nestbox species only, you can gain a permit more quickly, as a smaller range of skills is required. There is no fixed number of birds to have extracted, ringed or processed in order to achieve a ringing permit, rather the time needed to train will depend on aptitude and experience. For further information visit our website (www.bto.org/ringing).

When did ringing start?

Bird ringing for scientific purposes began in Denmark in 1899 when Hans Mortensen fitted 164 Starlings with metal rings engraved with successive numbers and a return address. The first British & Irish ringing schemes were started in 1909 by Harry Witherby in connection with the journal

The first bird that was ringed in Britain & Ireland and reported overseas was a Common Tern that was found in northwest Spain in September 1909, two months after it was ringed.

British Birds and (independently) by Arthur Landsborough Thomson in Aberdeen. The Aberdeen scheme came to an end during the First World War (although Sir Arthur Landsborough Thomson remained closely associated with bird ringing), while the Witherby scheme was transferred to the recently-formed British Trust for Ornithology in 1937. Bird ringing schemes have since developed in many parts of the world (Chapter 1).

What and when were the first birds ringed by the BTO Ringing Scheme?
The first birds in what became the BTO Ringing Scheme were ringed on Saturday 8 May 1909 at Sands of Forvie in Aberdeenshire, Scotland. One of those birds, Lapwing AU32, subsequently became the first bird to be recaught on 13 June 1909 close to the site where it was ringed (the report of this bird is shown in Chapter 2).

What were the first international recoveries involving Britain & Ireland?
The first record of a bird ringed in Britain & Ireland and found abroad was a Common Tern. It was ringed as a chick on 30 July 1909 in Ravenglass, Cumbria, and found exhausted in A Coruña, northwestern Spain on 21 September 1909.

The first bird ringed overseas that was found in Britain & Ireland was a Pintail. The bird was ringed on 20 October 1908 on Fanø, Denmark and shot on 20 November 1908 on the Dornoch Firth in Highland. A second Pintail ringed at the same time was found on 15 April 1909 at Lough Neagh in County Tyrone.

How many birds are ringed?
In Europe it is estimated that a total of 115 million birds have been ringed during the 20th Century. To date more than 36 million birds have been

JILL PAKENHAM

The first birds ringed in Britain & Ireland were Lapwings ringed in Aberdeenshire in May 1909. One of these birds became the first recovery when it was found the following month.

ringed in Britain & Ireland; between them, BTO ringers typically ring 800,000 birds a year. The most-ringed species are Blue Tit, Greenfinch and Blackbird. The 10 bird species with the highest number of ringed individuals are shown in the record breakers section below.

How many birds are recovered?

The total number of birds recovered in Europe during the 20th Century is more than 2 million. Each year BTO HQ receives around 14,000 reports of ringed birds that have been found dead or have been recaught by ringers at least 5 km away from the ringing site. Common causes of death are shown in the table on page 74. Thousands more birds are also retrapped alive by ringers close to the site where they were ringed.

How far do birds travel?

The map shows some of the longest movements by birds ringed in Britain & Ireland. Of the long-distance migrants, terns are amongst the longest-lived, so will fly a great distance during their lifetime. For example, the oldest ringed Common Tern may have flown over 1.5 million km in its 33 years! However, Swifts spend ten months of the year on the wing, so probably beat this record – at almost 18 years, the oldest ringed Swift could easily have travelled more than 7 million km in its lifetime! Examples of ringed birds that have lived the longest and travelled the furthest are in the tables on pages 71 & 72. The record for the longest single flight belongs to Alaskan Bar-tailed Godwits, which fly non-stop across the Pacific to New Zealand, a journey of around 10,000 km, which takes them about 10 days.

BOX 9 AMAZING JOURNEYS

Knot
4,324 km

Brent
Goose
5,443 km

Pochard
9,254 km

Manx
Shearwater
12,516 km

Arctic Tern
12,996 km

Arctic Tern
*Arctic Tern CK 10391 was
ringed on the Farne
Islands, Northumberland in
1961 (12,996 km).*
Arctic Terns are perhaps our
greatest migrants, and this bird
is our furthest south recovery.
It died when it hit a whaler in
a snowstorm. Another Arctic
Tern (CK51037) is our furthest
travelled bird, being found in
Australia, 18,056 km from home.

Manx Shearwater
*Manx Shearwater FB02701
was ringed on Sanda Island,
Strathclyde in 2000 (12,516 km).*
Most Manx Shearwaters breeding
in Britain & Ireland spend the
winter in the western South
Atlantic, so this recovery is
quite typical. A ringed Manx

Shearwater found in Australia,
though, was the first record of
this species for the country.

Pochard
*Pochard GM25413 was ringed in
Lincolnshire in 1966 (9,254 km).*
Many of our familiar ducks
are visitors from the east.
This Pochard found in eastern
Russia is an extreme example,
but shows how truly global our
birds are. Male Tufted Ducks
come to Britain & Ireland to
moult their flight feathers in
autumn - SS79184, ringed
in Essex in 1969 was later
found in Pakistan.

Brent Goose
*Brent Goose GP86247 was
ringed in Essex in 1976
(5,443 km).*

Brent Geese from two different
populations winter in Britain &
Ireland, the light-bellied and the
dark-bellied. This bird was from
the dark-bellied population,
which breeds in the open
tundra, as far east as the
Taimyr peninsula in the central
Russian Arctic.

Knot
*Knot XR 13820 was ringed on
South Uist in 1985 (4,324 km).*
Virtually all Knot wintering
in Britain & Ireland breed in
Greenland and Arctic Canada.
This individual is a good
example of how far away these
birds can breed. It was caught
(and released) while incubating
four eggs on a nest at Polar
Bear Pass in the Northwest
Territories of Canada.

MARK GRANTHAM

How can I find out more about BTO?

There is a wealth of information about the work of the BTO on our website (www.bto.org) or contact BTO HQ (see back cover). You can find out more about individual species by looking at BirdFacts (www.bto.org/birdfacts) and the Breeding Birds in the Wider Countryside Report (www.bto.org/birdtrends). We organise a range of surveys each year and are always keen to have new volunteers to help. See Chapter 5 for more information.

What is EURING?

EURING (the European Union for Bird Ringing) aims to promote and encourage scientific studies and the use of ringing data for the management and conservation of birds in Europe and further afield (see www.euring.org for more information). Reports of ringed birds that have been gathered by bird ringing schemes throughout Europe are held in the EURING Data Bank (EDB), and EURING welcomes applications from researchers to analyse particular data sets (www.euring.org/data_and_codes/obtaining_data).

How can I find out more about migration?

Movements of birds from Britain & Ireland are explored in-depth in the *Migration Atlas*, which brings together the knowledge gained from bird ringing since 1909. These findings are summarised in an easy-to read book called *Time to Fly* (see Further Reading at the end of Chapter 5). If you are a birdwatcher and have access to the Internet, please consider submitting your records to BirdTrack, a year-round online bird recording scheme developed through a partnership between BTO, RSPB and BirdWatch Ireland (www.birdtrack.net), which allows us to map the migration and movements of birds and monitor scarce birds in Britain & Ireland.

RECORD BREAKERS

The oldest ringed bird

Seabirds, waterfowl and waders tend to live longer than songbirds. The oldest bird in the Ringing Scheme so far is a Manx Shearwater ringed at Bardsey Bird Observatory in North Wales on 17 May 1957. It has been recaught on several occasions, the most recent being 8 May 2008, making it over 50 years old. Records for the 10 oldest songbirds are shown opposite. Longevity records (of more than a year) for all species ringed in Britain & Ireland can be found on the BTO website (www.bto.org/ringing/ringinfo/longevity.htm). Longevity records for birds ringed all over Europe are shown on the EURING website (www.euring.org/data_and_codes/longevity.htm).

The oldest bird in the Ringing Scheme is this Manx Shearwater ringed at Bardsey Bird Observatory in North Wales on 17 May 1957, when it was already an adult. It was recaught on 8 May 2008, making it over 50 years old!

STEVEN STANSFIELD: WILDLIFEIMAGES

Oldest ringed bird species

SPECIES	DATE RINGED	DATE FOUND	TIME BETWEEN RINGING AND FINDING
1 Manx Shearwater	17 May 1957	08 May 2008	50 years, 11 months, 22 days
2 Razorbill	02 Jul 1962	25 Jun 2004	41 years, 11 months, 23 days
3 Fulmar	18 Jul 1951	03 Jun 1992	40 years, 10 months, 16 days
4 Pink-footed Goose	29 Oct 1959	05 Jun 1998	38 years, 7 months, 7 days
5 Gannet	15 Jul 1961	01 Dec 1998	37 years, 4 months, 16 days
6 Oystercatcher	29 Aug 1969	15 May 2006	36 years, 8 months, 16 days
7 Eider	06 Oct 1958	02 May 1994	35 years, 6 months, 26 days
8 Lesser Black-backed Gull	03 Jul 1965	30 May 2000	34 years, 10 months, 27 days
9 Wigeon	15 Feb 1962	15 Sep 1996	34 years, 7 months, 0 days
10 Common Tern	01 Jul 1963	07 Jul 1996	33 years, 0 months, 6 days

Oldest ringed songbird species

SPECIES	DATE RINGED	DATE FOUND	TIME BETWEEN RINGING AND FINDING
1 Rook	01 May 1982	01 Apr 2005	22 years, 11 months, 0 days
2 Magpie	17 May 1925	09 Feb 1947	21 years, 8 months, 23 days
3 Raven	08 May 1982	23 Apr 2000	17 years, 11 months, 15 days
4 Crow	08 Jun 1981	19 Apr 1999	17 years, 10 months, 11 days
5 Starling	20 Nov 1983	15 Jul 2001	17 years, 7 months, 25 days
6 Jay	24 Sep 1966	13 Jul 1983	16 years, 9 months, 19 days
7 Chough	20 Mar 1965	16 Dec 1981	16 years, 8 months, 26 days
8 Jackdaw	22 May 1985	08 May 2001	15 years, 11 months, 16 days
9 Blackbird	14 Jun 1937	15 Aug 1951	14 years, 2 months, 1 days
10 Great Tit	23 May 1976	28 Apr 1990	13 years, 11 months, 5 days

The longest distance
The 10 species ringed in Britain & Ireland that have travelled the furthest.

SPECIES	COUNTY RINGED	COUNTRY FOUND	DISTANCE TRAVELLED (KM)
1 Arctic Tern	Anglesey	Australia	18,056
2 Common Tern	Co Down	Australia	17,641
3 Manx Shearwater	Dyfed	Australia	16,675
4 Storm Petrel	Shetland	South Africa	10,839
5 Arctic Skua	Shetland	South Africa	10,719
6 Swallow	Highland	South Africa	10,552
7 Sandwich Tern	Orkney	South Africa	10,508
8 Spotted Flycatcher	Gwynedd	South Africa	10,015
9 Knot	Norfolk	South Africa	9,921
10 Sanderling	Norfolk	South Africa	9,820

The most ringed
The top 10 species ringed in Britain & Ireland.

SPECIES	NUMBER RINGED*
1 Blue Tit (right)	3,268,768
2 Greenfinch	1,989,549
3 Blackbird	1,819,514
4 Swallow	1,717,776
5 Great Tit	1,611,887
6 Starling	1,343,412
7 Willow Warbler	1,216,834
8 Chaffinch	1,158,538
9 Sand Martin	1,118,279
10 Robin	889,189

JILL PAKENHAM

*to the end of 2007

Highest recovery rate
The 10 species (of which more than 1,000 individuals have been ringed) with the highest rate of recoveries (reports of ringed birds).

SPECIES	NUMBER RINGED	NUMBER REPORTED	RECOVERY RATE (%)
1 Bewick's Swan	2,416	1,346	55.7
2 Pink-footed Goose	15,095	4,709	31.2
3 Mute Swan	114,183	29,859	26.2
4 White-fronted Goose	2,432	574	23.6
5 Greylag Goose	12,449	2,890	23.2
6 Whooper Swan	2,775	575	20.7
7 Canada Goose	74,270	12,735	17.1
8 Eider	22,806	3,692	16.2
9 Shoveler	2,962	475	16.0
10 Mallard	175,569	26,311	15.0

GEORGE H. HIGGINBOTHAM

BTO HQ has received several reports of Black-headed Gulls that have been hit by flying golf balls!

Most unusual recoveries

SPECIES	PLACE & DATE RINGED	PLACE & DATE FOUND	CIRCUMSTANCES
Osprey	Strathclyde 14 Jul 1998	The Gambia 19 Nov 2000	Ring found in the stomach of a crocodile
Mute Swan	Cheshire 17 Dec 1995	Chester Zoo 12 Feb 1997	Killed by tigers
Reed Warbler	Kent 21 Aug 2001	Guinea Bissau 13 Oct 2001	Found in a large spider web
Two Mute Swans and a Great Black-backed Gull	Various parts of Britain	Various parts of Britain	Trampled by cows
5 Black-headed Gulls, a Mallard and a Canada Goose	One gull ringed in Denmark, one in Norway, all others in Britain	Various parts of Britain	Hit (and killed) by golf balls

Fastest birds

Although it is difficult to measure the speed that birds travel, examples of some of the fastest movements of ringed birds are shown below.

SPECIES	PLACE & DATE RINGED	PLACE & DATE FOUND	DISTANCE TRAVELLED (KM)	NO. OF DAYS BETWEEN RINGING AND FINDING
Gadwall (3 individuals)	Dunkirk, Cambridgeshire 27 Jan 2003	Landrecies, northern France 27 Jan 2003	352	Same day
Goldcrest	Sjaelland, Denmark 17 Oct 1990	Humberside 18 Oct 1990	737	One day
Swallow	Icklesham, Sussex 14 Oct 1998	Liberia, West Africa 23 Oct 1998	4,932	Nine days

Most frequently recovered foreign-ringed birds

The 10 species ringed abroad that have been most frequently recovered in Britain & Ireland.

	SPECIES	NUMBER REPORTED
1	Black-headed Gull	11,076
2	Starling	4,412
3	Dunlin	4,024
4	Teal	3,153
5	Pink-footed Goose	2,629
6	Blackbird	1,920
7	Common Gull	1,760
8	Chaffinch	873
9	Storm Petrel	867
10	Mediterranean Gull	827

Causes of mortality

Below are some of the common causes of mortality from dead ringed birds that are found, most of them attributed to humans! However, in many cases where a bird is found dead the cause of mortality is unknown. Minimum numbers are shown.

	CAUSE	NUMBER
1	Hunted, trapped or poisoned	132,500+
2	Shot	84,000+
3	Taken by cat	41,900+
4	Hit by a car	34,900+
5	Collision with window	13,800+
6	Collision with overhead wires	9,400+
7	Oil	5,600+
8	Raptor kills	5, 300+
9	Pollution (excluding oil)	1,500+
10	Collision with man-made structure	1,000+

We are very grateful to The Wetland Trust and Porzana Ltd for financial support for this Guide, as well as their continued supply of high-quality rings.

The Ringing and Nest Record Schemes are funded by a partnership of the British Trust for Ornithology, the Joint Nature Conservation Committee (on behalf of Natural England, Scottish Natural Heritage and the Countryside Council for Wales, and also on behalf of the Environment and Heritage Service in Northern Ireland). The Ringing Scheme is also funded by The National Parks and Wildlife Service (Ireland) and the ringers themselves.

We are grateful to everyone whose research projects we featured in the book. In particular: Black-tailed Godwit movements – Jennifer Gill, UEA; Bittern movements – Gillian Gilbert, RSPB; Osprey movements – Roy Dennis, Highland Foundation for Wildlife; EURING Swallow Project – Fernando Spina. The figure that appears in Box 7 (EURING Swallow Project) was modified from Rubolini, D., Pastor, A.G., Pilastro, A. & Spina, F. (2002) Ecological barriers shaping fuel stores in Barn Swallows *Hirundo rustica* following the central and western Mediterranean flyways. *Journal of Avian Biology* 33, 15-22. Blackwell Publishing Ltd.

Thank you to all the photographers who have allowed us to use their excellent illustrations, which have added so much to the book. We are particularly grateful to Derek Robertson, who designed our fantastic centenary logo.

Thanks to Alan Martin, Dave Coker, Dorian Moss and Natasha Atkins, who made useful comments on earlier drafts of the Guide. We are grateful for the support and help of our colleagues in the Ringing Scheme and other BTO staff who were always ready to help out. Dave Leech wrote the Nest Record Scheme text and Mark Grantham produced the maps. Jane Waters, as always, cheerfully provided excellent secretarial support – often at short notice.

We would like to thank the Trustees of the Natural History Museum for continuing permission to use their address on BTO rings and for forwarding reports of ringed birds to us. Thanks are also due to our colleagues in other ringing schemes around the world, for their support and cooperation.

We are especially grateful to everyone who has found a ringed bird and reported it to the BTO.

Finally, most thanks go to the many ringers, both past and present, whose enthusiasm, dedication, hard work and expertise have led to the success of the BTO Ringing Scheme and continue to further our knowledge of the birds of Britain & Ireland.